DETERMINED

(To Ride that Train to Success)

Kelvin Daniels

NEWMAN SPRINGS PUBLISHING
320 Broad Street
Red Bank, NJ 07701

First originally published by Newman Springs Publishing 2024

ISBN 979-8-89061-987-7 (Paperback)
ISBN 979-8-89061-988-4 (Digital)

Printed in the United States of America

In memory of my parents, I dedicate this book and all inspiring words, as well as encouragements, that my parents gave me through the years. Because of the strong family values, the undying love that was shown, and a solid base understanding of how much God moves in our lives, is a true testament to how proud they would be today. Their loving, caring, sincere personalities, I carry each day of my life.

Today, my parents have both passed on from this earthly world. I, too, one day have to close my eyes and pay my debt from this earthly world, and I look forward to one day seeing all my loved ones again on the other side.

CONTENTS

PREFACE

Growing up as an inner-city youth in New York City, I developed a prominent law enforcement career. This is a train ride taking me down the tracks, telling the story of my life, and carrying me to places where I had much success in this journey. A journey that taught me patience, understanding, and how to make a difference in society. All this gave me much joy and happiness.

DADDY

There aren't enough words
   to say what I feel in my
      heart for you,

But you seem to say just
   what I feel in everything
      you say and do.

It's love you've always shown
   me and how very much you care

No matter how big or small
   my problems were, you were
      always there

To give me hope to hold my
   hand to do any and everything
      you can

From the bottom of my heart
   I give you many thanks
      and I thank God too, for
         giving me life and most of
            all for giving me to you.

MY EARLY MORNING PRAYER

Must Jesus bear the cross alone, and all the world go free? No, there's a cross for everyone; there's a cross for me. Father, once again, I want to thank you for opening up my eyes to see another day, a day that I have never seen before, but an opportunity to make changes in my life for the better. So many eyes did not open this morning, but you saw fit to let my moments roll on just a little while longer. Thank you, Father. Thank you for being so good and merciful to me.

I ask you to put a special blessing on my family, friends, and all people, wherever they may be. Bless those that are sick, those in hospitals, nursing homes, and institutions, wherever they may be. Put a very special blessing on those who have lost a loved one. Let them know and feel your presence by their side. Father, one thing for sure is that you don't make any mistakes. When we come to the end of our journey, you pick your flowers according to your wishes, not ours. As sure as we are living, we all have to one day face that same fate.

Father, touch this day, and please let your guardian angels keep all hurt, harm, and dangers from around me. This is my prayer. Hear my prayer, O Lord. Hear my prayer, O Lord. Incline thy ear to us and grant us thy peace. Amen.

Elder John Wallace Daniels
1921–2007
Went Home to Glory

First Lady, Fannie L. Daniels
1932–2012
The Queen of Our Family

CHAPTER 1

Early Years

In the evening of March 12, 1962, 7:00 p.m., I was born. I was born in Mount Vernon Hospital, Mount Vernon, New York. Mount Vernon is a midsize city located in Westchester County in the state of New York. Westchester County actually neighbors the borough of the Bronx, which is located in the city of New York.

I was the third of three children. I had one brother and one sister. My brother passed away a few years ago. I miss him dearly. He taught me a lot

Growing up in the '60s, '70s, and '80s were good years. My family, along with so many other families, did not have a whole lot of materialistic things, but the one thing we had was a lot of love and quality family time for each other. I remember very often how I would go outside and throw a ball up against this empty shack that was in front of where we lived and catch the ball as it would return to me after it bounced off the wall. It taught me how to catch. From that, I developed very good hand skills. I played catch with this ball many times for many days. This was part of entertaining yourself, by yourself.

Every now and then, my parents would let me go down the street to the playground in the neighborhood. My parents told my brother, by him being older than me, to keep a watchful eye on me so that no one would bother me or I couldn't get into any type of trouble. In that particular park, there always seemed to be this basketball there that didn't bounce much because of lack of air. But I didn't have a pump or access to one, so I just kept trying to shoot the ball in the goal as best as I could.

I learned the game of basketball this way, and this way surely kept my attention. In later years, learning this way really turned out to be very rewarding. In those years, you made the most of whatever resources you could come up with. In New York, we played a lot of different sports according to the season outside. In the winter times when we had snow, and at times a lot of snow, I would get with some of my friends in the neighborhood and we would have big snowball fights. When we got tired of having snowball fights, my friends and I would go over to the hill on the next street over and slide down the hill using garbage can tops. That was a lot of fun.

That same hill we used to ride our go-carts. My friends and I would go around in our neighborhoods and see what people would put out to the curbs for excess junk. That's where we would find the materials to build our go-carts. After we would put together one, we would build another until we all had one. Then we would go to the hill and test the go-carts out for speed and accuracy. Those days bring back a lot of memories.

Some days when the weather outside was bad and I didn't go out to play, I would be in the house watching our 13-inch black-and-white television, or I would be playing my record player with the few records that I had. Most of the time, we watched television as a family. On certain nights, TV shows like *Sanford and Son*, *Chico and the Man*, or *The Flip Wilson Show* were popular family-watched shows at that time. I also liked *Adam-12* and *Gentle Ben*.

Family time was a very important time. We ate our meals daily all together as a family, always thanking God for our food before we ate. God is so good and merciful. He blesses us in so many ways. I always said my prayers each night before I got into bed, always being thankful to God, asking him to watch over me, my family, and mankind everywhere as we lay down to sleep.

Music was something that I enjoyed listening to as well. I played a few instruments myself, the trombone and the drums. Music in the '60s was so different from how it is today. Artists wrote about and sung about life and family experiences. Most importantly, you could understand the music. Musicians actually came out onto the stages and played their instruments in the '60s. The Jackson Five, *Soul Train*, and *American Bandstand* were very popular. Most of my friends were wearing Afros.

Chuck Taylor Converse Sneakers were the popular footwear. The ABA basketball league, American Basketball Association, had the red, white, and blue basketball. My friends and I would watch the basketball games on TV during the weekends and then go outside to the playgrounds and imitate those moves that we had seen those basketball stars do on TV.

Hamilton Elementary School was the first school that I attended. I really enjoyed going to school there. I made many friends, some of which I still keep in contact with today. In the mornings before school took in for the day, we, the students, would gather around in the schoolyard and do what we called back then running the bases. The bases were in the form of a baseball field diamond: first base, second base, third base, and then home plate. This is how the race would go: two people would face opposite directions at home plate. When someone would announce "Go," one person would start toward first, second, third, and back to home plate, while the other person would start toward third, second, first, and then to home plate. Whoever crossed home plate first was declared the winner. That's how we could determine who the fastest person in the school was at this time. Running the bases was a daily game that we played whenever we were in the playground.

Fourth Avenue in Mount Vernon was our shopping center. It was back then as it is much like today compared to shopping malls. There were all types of clothing stores, shoe stores, restaurants, supermarkets, and one of my favorite stores was the pet shop. During those days, you could see all types of different puppies and kittens in the front windows of the pet shop. My first pet was a cat. I named her Bobbi. We had her for several years. She stayed inside our apartment until one day, she got out. We later found out when she returned that she was going to have kittens. She did. She had six kittens, much too much for an apartment. We gave the kittens away and then had her spayed.

CHAPTER 2

Moving to the City

At ten years old, my family decided to move to the Bronx, New York. The Bronx is one of the five boroughs in the city of New York. Moving from Mount Vernon to the Bronx was definitely a big change. The borough of the Bronx has over two and a half million people there alone. You have a whole lot more things going on there. For example, the famous Bronx Zoo, a real zoo in a residential neighborhood and one of the oldest zoos in the United States. You have theaters, all kinds of parks, shopping places all over. If something is to be found, it can be found in the city of New York.

We settled down in a place called Co-op City. Co-op City is truly just what it sounds like: 35 high-rise buildings, 7 townhouse clusters, 15,372 apartments, 5 different sections with a population of 50,000 people. Buildings range from 22 floors to 33 floors depending on where you are living. Each section has its own shopping centers and parking garages. There were 2 elementary schools, 2 intermediate schools, and 1 high school there, Harry S. Truman High School, for the residents. Harry S. Truman High School looked just like a castle and was 7 stories high with a capacity of 4,000 students. Even though there were a lot of people, you still made a lot of friends. There were many days that my friends and I would just get together and go to other sections of Co-op City that we didn't always get a chance to go to because we live in other sections.

Pizza is one of my favorite dishes along with lasagna and spaghetti. I also like seafood. Pizza restaurants seem like they are everywhere in New York. White Castle has a franchise for the best little square hamburgers that don't cost you that much. Nathan's hot dogs are the best beef hot dogs, to me, that you can buy along with Hebrew National beef hot dogs. City Island, just outside of Co-op City offers all types of seafood for the seafood lover. McDonald's, Burger King, Popeyes Chicken, Wendy's, and many other food restaurants are all over the city. Whatever food you like, it's there in New York City for you to enjoy. Some days, my friends and I would just get on the subway trains and take a ride. We would just pick a stop and get off and see what stores and eating places were around. There's always something new in New York City that you possibly have not seen before. No matter where my friends and I might go, we all always knew that we had to be back home when it was time to eat. Mealtime was definitely family time. Families today, for the most part, don't sit down and eat with one another daily like we used to back then. People's morals today have surely changed tremendously. The love, compassion, and understanding are almost nonexistent.

In those days, you would see a man, while in a restaurant, pull the lady's chair out for her to sit down. At times, you would see a man, if he was wearing a hat, tip his hat to a lady when introduced to her. Not to mention opening up the car door for your lady when she was entering or exiting a vehicle. These were things that I was raised on. My father demonstrated these things all the time with my mother. He was teaching me then how to be a young man and then develop into a mature man who had a good strong upbringing. I thank him so much right to this day.

My parents were both born and raised in North Carolina. My grandparents had already laid down the roots for my parents to follow. Prayer, Sunday school, and participating in church were surely a must in our household. My parents always said, "God has been too good in our lives for us not to give him some of our time in return," and that meant worshiping him. Both of my parents worked and retired from the city of New York. We had a family truck that I worked on several days a week, preferably after attending school for the day. It was a food truck on wheels. My father had it converted over to everything that would be in the average restaurant. I didn't know then how instrumental that truck would be in my life. It taught me values that I would use through my adolescent years, right to my adult years.

Growing up and all through life, my parents stressed a good education, having a strong work ethic, treating people right, and a good Christian base. Sometimes you run into many obstacles, but you don't let that deter you. You just continue to try hard. You can achieve; just stay focused. My parents had one golden rule: Put God first in everything that you try to achieve. Let him guide you and he will see you through. In some cases, he will deter us from something that we think might be good for us and they are not. God knows our beginnings, middle, and endings, far before we know them ourselves. Always remember that.

I went out to the park one day and was playing on this big outside gym set, running, jumping, and swinging on the monkey bars. That's when I met six of my best friends of today. We played together daily. We walked to school every day to and from school. We went all over the city very often, but always the seven of us were primarily together. Each of our parents were good friends, as well as us. We did not know this then, but the seven of us would remain the best of friends for over fifty years. We used to go to the pizza restaurant and put all our money together and get two slices of pizza and have it cut so that we all could get some, along with two sodas and seven small cups. We shared everything because no one had a lot of money back in those days. A dollar was a dollar then.

Occasionally, we would go over to the supermarket, Pathmark, and help people leaving the supermarket carry their groceries to their vehicles for tips. We could always make a few dollars doing that. From time to time, we would eat lunch and sometimes dinner at each other's houses, after first getting permission from our parents. In the city, different things that kids could do were constantly coming out. We learned to ride unicycles, we learned to ride skateboards, we played backgammon, we played stickball, as well as handball. We all definitely bounced the rock and played basketball. On the weekends in the park, the older men in the neighborhood came out and played basketball in the courts. We sat on the sidelines and watched them play.

In 1976, one of the men who came out on the weekend to play ball with the older men had a heart attack and died. The older men who he played with on the weekends came together and came up with the idea of starting a basketball tournament in honor of their friend. That was the beginning of the Jerome Pickett Memorial Tournament. It was a tournament that was divided into different age brackets, an age bracket for everyone in the community who wished to participate. The first year, it cost $2 a player, $20 a team. That was the cost for the T-shirt and trophy. Today, that tournament has a registration price of over $300 a team. It's one of the biggest basketball tournaments in New York, highly recognized just as much as Harlem's Rucker or City-Wide.

Basketball is definitely a big thing in New York City. Some of the best basketball players come out of these tournaments. I played in different tournaments every year all around the city. I won a lot of championships and met a lot of people. There, in Co-op City, I attended Intermediate School #180, Dr. Daniel Hale Williams. Our rival school was Intermediate School #181. We constantly were competing against one another in sports. Every year, when school was out for the summer, my parents would let me come down south to North Carolina for a few weeks to spend some time with some of my family members there. I had a lot of relatives on my father's side as well as on my mother's side, considering that they were both born and raised in North Carolina.

I enjoyed seeing the different animals. Gave me a chance to go and do some fishing with my cousins. The air was even fresher in the south, no pollution from the tall buildings for a change. Eating the different fresh foods grown from the gardens was even nice. A lot of the foods that we ate in New York came out of a can instead of being freshly grown from the gardens. The country streets were dirt streets in a lot of cases, compared to the cement streets in New York everywhere. Getting used to everyone speaking to each other, as opposed to passing by people on the streets in NYC, not speaking but only to the people that you know.

Now there is nothing like a good hot slice of New York–style pizza, compared to a barbecue sandwich with coleslaw in the south, North Carolina. After a few weeks in the south with my relatives and friends, it was return time back to the city. Through the years, I made many trips from New York to North Carolina on the Trailways or Greyhound bus lines. By this time back in the city, the basketball tournaments were now beginning and soon would be in full swing. I surely was looking forward to playing ball with my friends again. It seemed like every year the tournaments got better and more challenging. Our games got better each year as we were getting older. It's true, practice does make perfect. We played ball with each other very often. That's the beauty about New York City, there are no two days just alike. There's always something different to do. One statement that holds very true about New York is, "Whether it's the city, which consists of one of the five boroughs, Manhattan, Bronx, Queens, Brooklyn, or Staten Island, you can never visit every part of New York State." Too many places to go and see. Too many shopping places to shop. That's what keeps New York so interesting. A true city that never sleeps. Something always going on twenty-four hours a day. There's also a lot of temptation that the city brings. That's when you have to remember what's right and what's wrong. My best friends and I hung around each other daily.

My friends and I always watched out for one another. The crime aspect of being raised within the inner city comes down to a matter of the choices that you make. You can choose to participate or avoid the bad elements. I understood that then, as well as today, you have in a lot of cases "peer pressures." In my specific case, that's where good friends kicked in. The people that you associate with have a big bearing on what's happening around you. If you're associating with people who have positive goals in life, then you really don't have time for getting into trouble. If you're associating with people who break the laws of the land, stealing, robbing people, gang activities, selling drugs, being disrespectful to elders and your parents, just to mention a few things, these bad traits will end you up in one or two places: jail, prison, or the cemetery. My best friends and I have been best friends for over fifty years to this day. Our parents were just as close as we were good friends. Choices, chances, and consequences speak volumes about growing up in the inner city or the State of New York. Your parents work very hard to provide for us. The least thing that we can do is not to put on them any unnecessary burdens that don't make any reasonable sense. Raising a family and keeping it strong is tough enough right by itself. I appreciate my parents dearly, and I appreciated my friends' parents as well. I knew that their parents would only tell me things to help me and guide me in the right way in life.

My family and I always had family discussions at the kitchen table no matter how big or small the topic was. It was discussed by the family. My parents always stressed honesty regardless of what the topic of discussion was. Therefore, I didn't have to worry if there was something bothering me and I didn't have anyone to talk to. That was never the case. My parents, as well as my best friend's parents, always had time for me and us. You see young children today getting into all kinds of trouble. I personally feel that a lot of things didn't have to be if there was just someone that they felt that they could talk to or just get some good advice from. My parents always made sure that we lived in a good environment and kept me participating in positive programs going on in the neighborhood. Going to school back then in the '70s and '80s, your parents, uncles, and aunts were subject to show up at your school and come in for a visit. Your loved ones wanted to see what you were learning and also how you were behaving in your classrooms. I realize in this day and time, the school systems don't allow those types of unannounced visits to the schools anymore, but they should. Those visits kept down a whole lot of bad behavior in the classrooms as well as within the school.

How it was now (1976), graduating time from the eighth grade (IS #180), going next door to Harry S. Truman High School. As I stated earlier, the elementary schools, PS #151 and PS #153, along with IS #180, IS #181, and then Harry S. Truman High School, were all there in the same complex.

That's what made Co-op City so special. Even though the schools were big and had a lot of students, you still had a chance to learn and meet a lot of people. One thing about going to schools in the city is you have a lot of opportunities to go to other schools outside of your neighborhoods. For example, if you're gifted in math or science, you can apply to the Bronx High School of Science. If you have a special gift of dancing, arts, or music, you can apply to the School of the Arts. There are other schools there as well. I attended Harry S. Truman High School for a couple of years, and then my parents decided that we would be moving south to North Carolina, after my parents decided that they were going to have a house built there. That was truly a drastic change for me. Leaving my friends, leaving the city lifestyle, was a real big deal. You're talking about a major change, but I had to adapt because that's where my parents said that we were going to be moving to.

When I arrived in North Carolina and saw my new home, being around family and meeting new people at school, then it wasn't so bad after all. I was enrolled into D. H. Conley High School. It wasn't as big as the high school that I was accustomed to seeing in New York City, but I was looking forward to a new beginning in North Carolina. People are a lot friendlier in the south, and that was very refreshing. I had my own basketball court in the backyard of my house. I really liked that.

Now all I had to do was find out who had basketball skills in the neighborhood and at school. My basketball game was tight. I've been playing ball ever since I was eight years old. My brother taught me what he knew, and he was very good. I had played in NYC Harlem Rucker, City-Wide, Big Mac Classic, and Jerome Pickett Memorial Tournament. When basketball tryouts came around in school, I tried out and made the team. One thing that I quickly liked was the food being served in the cafeteria. It was very good, and they gave you plenty. The teachers were great. They really cared about you getting the best quality education possible. That drive was so important then, just as it is still important today. Teachers really set the foundation for shaping the students for a potentially bright future. Every year is a stepping stone to what you can achieve. The sky is definitely the limit, but that extra push always can help make a difference. Farming at this time was the big industry in the south. I personally didn't know anything about farming, but a lot of my classmates now grew up and worked on the farm, some of them since they were very young. Farming included at that time tobacco, corn, harvesting cucumbers, peas, cotton, and raising pigs and chickens, just to mention a few things. It surely was a big lifestyle change for me to see, but very interesting. I had a large family in North Carolina, and several of my uncles, aunts, cousins, and neighbors had farm animals right there in their yards behind their homes.

Raising pigs and chickens especially was a way of feeding your families. Several times I had an opportunity to watch my uncles, who raised pigs, prepare a pig in order to be slaughtered. You raise a piglet to a pig and then a pig to a hog. That's when he is ready to be slaughtered. My uncles would go out to the hog pen, select a few hogs, and slaughter them. After washing them and cleaning them, they would put them over this big pit that was dug in the ground and cook them for several hours. There was a lot of meat on that hog that could feed a family for quite a while.

My aunts raised chickens. Every morning, they would go out to the chicken coop and gather the eggs that the hens had laid overnight. That meant fresh eggs on the morning table for breakfast. My aunts also would catch several chickens in the chicken coop and wring the chicken's neck until it came off. Then my aunts would pull off the feathers, wash the chickens, and then prepare them to be cooked. That was either for lunch or dinner. Food then was freshly grown and naturally fed. Just about everyone in the community had a garden around their homes. Fresh vegetables being grown was a delight when you're used to getting most of your vegetables in a can in the city.

In the summertime, most of the children in the community were working with somebody who had a farm. I had never worked on a farm, but I decided this summer I would give it a try. Now I just had to find a farmer who would give me a chance to learn how to work on a farm since I had no experience. My parents knew someone who would give me a chance.

I was thankful to him for giving me the opportunity. This farmer had a tobacco farm. So that's what I was going to be working in, tobacco. It was very challenging but rewarding. I had to get up really early in the morning, but I was used to getting up early with my father while working on our family food truck. At an early age, it taught me responsibility in how to get a job and work that job as best as you possibly can. Good working ethics is an important aspect of being able to take care of your responsibilities in life, whether it's yourself or even your family. Being a responsible adult requires a few things: being able to find and keep employment, to have adequate transportation, and to maintain a place to live. Three things that a responsible adult must maintain. I learned this lesson early in life. Even though I was working, I still had time in the afternoons to play my favorite game of basketball. Many times at home, my parents would come outside in the backyard, sit in the lawn chairs, and watch me play. Dad and I would shoot around on the court, and Mom was the cheerleader. Playing ball outside gave us time to talk about various topics. We were a very close family. I had no secrets when it came down to my father and mother. My parents had a lot of love and understanding when it came to being about our family. A lot of things we take for granted in early years, but trust me, you will understand their teachings as you go along in life.

CHAPTER 3

My Heritage

My grandparents really set a strong path for our future family members to take. Being born in the late 1800s, they both went through a lot. Having a strong religious faith was really something that they had to hold on to. Slavery, racism, and plain simple meanness had to be endured. Ask yourself a question: was this fair? By no means, no. No person anywhere, regardless of their race, origin, or beliefs, should have to go through such horrible treatment. My grandparents still kept the family strong and raised and provided for my parents. At times, my father and mother would share many memories of the different situations that my grandparents taught them lessons. My grandfather and father would routinely go into the woods and use that large two-sided saw to cut down trees for wood to burn in the stove and to heat the house. They also would go out on a small boat and fish a lot for food for the family. My grandmother would do the cooking, sewing, and keeping things orderly around the house. Raising children back then was really more challenging than today because there really was a lot of everything less than it is compared to today. African American families have come a long way from the 1800s to 2021, but there still is a distant road ahead that we must get to. With God continuing to guide us, and only God, then that distant road is not impossible. Through the struggles, through the many tears, my grandparents made it through. They passed on a legacy to my parents, and in turn, my parents passed on that strong legacy to me. Thank God for wonderful grandparents.

My father was a very strong, soft-spoken man. He had a personality to achieve whatever he set out to do. Spiritual, a pastor of a church, a family man, sincere, and very respectful. He was my rock as well as being my role model. He had such patience and understanding. We had many father-and-son conversations. I always said and believed to myself, "If I could be just half of the man that my father was, then I would be satisfied." I was so proud of him being my father. He stressed many values then that I use today.

My mother was an easygoing, firm at times person. She wore a warm smile daily and displayed a very caring, Christian heart to everyone. Always trying to help somebody and brighten their day. She loved to bake our favorite desserts. Actually, my father and mother were quite a team in the kitchen. Both of my parents were awesome cooks, and they loved to cook. Every morning my mother would read from her Sunday schoolbook as well as from the Holy Bible. This she did after saying her daily prayers for the morning and before going to sleep at night. Both of my parents had a strong Christian base. They always said to me, "Whatever you try or want to do, put God first in the equation." Whatever concerts, sporting events, programs, etc. that we were involved in, both of my parents were right there in the audience, showing their support. That always meant so much to me. To have that type of support always would make our lives that much richer right by itself. Every day there was a full-course meal on the table for breakfast, lunch, and dinner. Also included was an afternoon snack for when we would come home from school. My parents believed in three full-course meals every day.

My mother would take a glass of milk, pour a pack of Carnation Instant Breakfast, along with a beaten egg, and have us drink that if we didn't want the traditional sausage and eggs treat with a side of oatmeal. She said that, that glass of milk gave us all the nutrients of a breakfast meal, and that was important for starting our day out at school. Those little things every day would later turn out to be major parts of all our lives. On Fridays, it was our family tradition, much like then and still to this day, seafood was for dinner with all of the __. Trout, whiting, shrimp, fish cakes, along with my father's homemade French fries and coleslaw was the meal.

There were many chores that we had to do around the home. For instance, vacuuming the floors in the house, cleaning the bathrooms, cleaning out the cars, and cutting the grass outside whenever it was needed. Even after accomplishing the tasks that needed to be done, there still was time for us to go outside and entertain ourselves.

We could take a simple ball back then and find different ways to get enjoyment from playing with it. Whether we threw it to each other, caught it, or just simply kicked it, we found a way to play with it.

Now the time was coming close when it was approaching graduation time from high school. I truly enjoyed my high school years. I met many friends.

CHAPTER 4

Putting the Pieces together

Chapter 5
High School and College Joining the US Army

I had a terrific staff that guided me along my pathway through high school. I had several career goals in mind, but I still had questions about which path to take. During my time in high school, I had a lot of things that I was interested in, such as carpentry, business law, science class, and sports. In carpentry class, we built a magazine rack. It was amazing using the different tools to make something from scratch. Business law class was interesting as well. You learned about the many aspects of starting a business, as well as what it took to maintain that business. That class really helped me for when I got out into the business world on my own. I learned that the classes you took in high school enabled you to use them in preparing you for what is to come in life.

I applied to different colleges that I had an interest in. I attended several orientations at several schools. I finally decided on Campbell University. Campbell University is located in Buies Creek, North Carolina. A liberal arts school with a law school also on the campus. A small college, with an enrollment that allowed for you to really interact with each other. My major course of study would be "Government." I wanted to learn all about politics and how politics worked. Campbell University was really another chapter in my life that prepared me very well for the future. After leaving Campbell University, I enlisted in the United States Army. Now, this was a big change from what my parents had hoped for me to do, but I had other career goals in mind.

AIRBORNE

One thing that I want to say is that education is a powerful tool, just as experience is equally a powerful tool. But college might not be for everyone. One thing you must have for whatever you are trying to achieve for the future is a *plan*. A plan entails whatever inspiration you have to have in order to make this an achievable goal. The sky is surely the limit to how high you can go, but you need the proper fuel to put into that rocket of success to gain your goal. For one, as I enlisted in the United States Army, that was the beginning of my law enforcement career. After basic training and advanced individual training, I became a military policeman with the 82nd Airborne Division. Being a military policeman gave me tremendous knowledge and experience. This was a beginning career that later in life, as well, would turn out to be very rewarding. I got a chance to travel, meet new people, and in many cases, made lifelong friends. Being in the military, in a lot of cases, gives you the independence that you need in developing young minds. It gives you a sense of much-needed purpose and true direction. Your responsibilities go to another level. That's the beauty of coming into your own as being a young adult.

There comes a time when my parents would say, "It's time to step out from the nest and be on your own." Hopefully, at this time, you are ready to begin to take on the world. Society at times can throw out some hard curves; that's when your teachings from your parents, uncles, and aunts begin to manifest. You can learn many things from many people every day of your life. Just keep an open mind.

Sometimes when the road gets a little rough for me, I think about some of those old hymns that I used to hear my parents sing while going through our house. One of my favorites was "My God is Real."

There are something __ I may not know,
There are some place I can't go,
But I am sure of this one thing,
That God is real for I can feel him deep with.

Some folk may doubt, some folk may scorn,
All can desert and leave me alone,
But as for me I'll take God's part,
For God is real and I can feel him in my heart.

I cannot tell just how you felt,
When Jesus took your sins away,
But since that day, yes, since that hour,
God has been real for I can feel his holy power

Verse:

Yes, God is real, real in my soul;
Yes, God is real for he has washed and made me whole;
His love for me is like pure gold,
Yes, God is real for I can feel him in my soul.

"His Eye Is on the Sparrow"

Why should I feel discouraged, why should the shadows come,
Why should my heart be lonely, and long for Heaven and home,
When Jesus is my portion? My constant Friend is He:
His eye is on the sparrow, and I know He watches me,
His eye is on the sparrow, and I know He watches me.

DETERMINED

Verse:

I sing because I'm happy, I sing because I'm free
For His eye is on the sparrow, and I know He watches me.

"Does Jesus Care?"

Does Jesus care when my heart is pained,
    Too deeply for mirth and song;
As the burdens press, and the cares distress,
    And the way grows weary and long?

Does Jesus care when my way is dark
    With a mameless dread and fear?
As the daylight fades into deep night shades,
    Does He care enough to be near?

Does Jesus care when I've tried and failed
    To resist some temptation strong,
When for my deep grief I find my relief,
    The tears flow all the night long?

Does Jesus care when I've said goodbye
    To the dearest on earth to me,
And my sad heart aches till it nearly breaks
    Is it aught to Him? Does He see?

Verse:

O yes, He cares. I know He cares.
His heart is touched with my grief;
When the days are weary, the long nights dreary,
I know my Savior cares.

During the times that my parents would be rejoicing, they would get so happy in themselves to a point where they seemed like they couldn't contain their own emotions. My father and mother always explained to me that one day, as long as you continue to live, when you look back over your life and see how God has worked in your life, then you could truly understand how you could get so happy. A lot of things we take for granted, not really thinking about the fact that our lives can change so quickly in a matter of minutes. Therefore, it really gives you an appreciation for God watching over my family, other people's families, and people all around the world, from their day-to-day activities. God is so good to everyone, even when we fall short about things ourselves. He's our constant protector. He's truly our awesome pilot in life for guiding us. He's truly also our best friend when we feel that all our other friends have possibly walked away. He will never leave you, nor forsake you, during any hour of the day.

As we live from day to day, give those love ones around us the hugs, the "I love yous," and express how much we appreciate what they have done in our lives. Because of the sacrifices our many loved ones have made for us, they made many of our far-reaching goals a reality. To make a convincing statement, our loved ones, paved the way for you as well as for me, and I truly do thank them.

CHAPTER 5

Law Enforcement on the Outside as Well as the Inside

After my first enlistment in the military, I decided to explore what other options were available for my future. After a brief dilemma, I became a police officer in my home state of New York. Being a Military Policeman in the United States Army really helped me tremendously in becoming a civilian police officer in New York. I was fortunate enough to work with and be trained by some of New York's best in the field of law enforcement. Growing up in New York gave me a jumpstart on the many types of personalities that I would be encountering on the job as a civilian police officer. There was much to learn, and I was very eager to learn what it took to be a good officer. New York is a fast and furious place, and so is being a law enforcement officer there. What I was taught would last me my entire career, and I want to thank my training officers and good partners for all their patience and diligence that they shared with me. My career got stronger and stronger as the years went along, leading to some very rewarding career changes. God truly was piloting my career, and I owe Him all the thanks and glory. Without Him guiding me along the way, none of my rewards would have ever been possible. If you put your trust and all your cares in His hands, He will lead you the right way. Yes, He will. I don't let a day go by without praising God's name. I never will forget from whence I came.

Included was an afternoon snack for when we would come home from school. My parents believed in 3 full-course meals every day.

My mother would take a glass of milk, pour a pack of Carnation Instant Breakfast along with a beaten egg, and have us drink that if we didn't want the traditional sausage and eggs treat with a side of oatmeal. She said that glass of milk gave us all the nutrients of a breakfast meal, and that was important for starting our day out at school. Those little things every day would later turn out to be major parts in all our lives. On Fridays, it was our family tradition, much like then and still to this day, seafood was for dinner with all the fixings. Trout, whiting, shrimp, fish cakes, along with my father's homemade French fries and coleslaw, was the meal.

There were many chores that we had to do around the home. For instance, vacuuming the floors in the house, cleaning the bathrooms, cleaning out the cars, and cutting the grass outside whenever it was needed. Even after accomplishing the tasks that needed to be done, there still was time for us to go outside and entertain ourselves. We could take a simple ball back then and find different ways to get enjoyment from playing with it. Whether we threw it to each other, caught it, or just simply kicked it, we found a way to play with it.

Now the time was coming close when it was approaching graduation time from high school. I truly enjoyed my high school years. I met many friends.

CHAPTER 6

Putting the Pieces Together

Chapter 5: High School and College Joining the U.S. Army

I had terrific staff that guided me along my pathway through high school. I had several career goals in mind but still had questions about which path to take. During my time in high school, I had a lot of things that I was interested in, such as carpentry, business law, science class, and sports. In Carpentry class, we built a magazine rack. It was amazing using the different tools to make something from scratch. Business law class was interesting as well. You learned about the many aspects of beginning a business, as well as what it took to maintain that business. That class really helped me when I got out into the business world on my own. I learned that the classes you took in high school enabled you to use them in preparing you for what is to come in life. I applied to different colleges that I had an interest in. I attended several orientations at several schools. I finally decided on Campbell University. Campbell University is located in Buies Creek, North Carolina. It is a liberal arts school with a law school also on the campus, a small college, with an enrollment that allowed for you to really interact with each other. My major course of study would be government. I wanted to learn all about politics and how politics worked. Campbell University was really another chapter in my life that prepared me very well for the future. After leaving Campbell University, I enlisted in the United States Army. Now this was a big change from what my parents had hoped for me to do, but I had other career goals in mind.

Now since I have good experience in being a military police and a police officer in New York, I wanted to expand my career even further. I wanted to learn the whole picture of the criminal justice system. I applied to the Department of Corrections and became a correctional officer. Being on the inside of a correctional institution was definitely going to be a challenge. It was a lot different from dealing with offenders on the streets. There again, I had good leadership teaching me how things were to go inside of a prison. One thing that I learned over time was that there is a big difference between being a police officer and being a correctional officer. Being a police officer, you do have the opportunity to deal with many situations outside of a facility, compared to being on an assigned post in a prison, where you have no outlet. Actually, being a correctional officer, you are doing "time" as well as the offenders doing time. You are unauthorized to leave an assigned post until you are properly relieved. That could be an eight-hour shift, ten-hour shift, or even a twelve-hour shift or even longer. I worked with the regular population inmates, mental health inmates, violently aggressive inmates, segregation units for disciplinary and administrative inmates, and prison emergency response team (for violent and unruly inmates). So as you can see, I worked all throughout the prison. I surely came up through my chain of command.

One Thursday afternoon in 2009, I received a telephone call from a doctor. He was a urologist. He asked me if I was Kelvin Daniels? and I said yes I am. He then told me who he was and informed me that I needed to come in and see him as soon as possible. I stated to him that I didn't know that I had a scheduled appointment to come in and see him. He said to me, "You don't have a scheduled appointment with me. I am making you an appointment now." I went the next day, Friday, to see him. When he came into my treatment room and informed me that I had cancer. The word *cancer* itself immediately took my feet from under my body. The word *cancer*, to me, was like giving me a death sentence. I sat in the treatment room for a while until I could get myself somewhat together. The initial shock was devastating. The doctor advised me that he wanted to do a biopsy, in order to see if the cancer was in a specific area or if it was all throughout my body. The cancer that I had was prostate cancer. That following Monday, the doctor did a biopsy and discovered that it was all in my prostate area. I went to the cancer center and had forty-two treatments of chemo and radiation. Eight weeks of treatments put my cancer into remission. I asked the doctor what would have happened if I never came in for treatment. He stated to me that in about a year, it would have taken *my life*. I was walking around each day working and doing my daily routine not knowing that I was carrying around cancer inside of my body.

Isn't God good? There were a lot of people in that cancer treatment room with me during my treatment time. Eighty percent of those people in that room with me at that time are no longer here alive today. They have paid their debt, which I still have to one day pay myself. Every day that we open our eyes is one day closer to closing them. God is truly our refuge and protector. He watches over us, even when we take so much for granted. He's our shelter in the midst of any storm. No matter what we may be going through, God will surely guide us through. Doctors may give us their professional opinion on what may be their prognosis, but God is the ultimate healer, and He needs no instructions. In my day-to-day journeys in my career, I challenge many people that I come in contact with to do something good for someone else other than yourself as often as you can. If you practice this task, God will bless you abundantly. You won't have enough room to receive all the blessings that He will pour out to you. You can't keep your hands so tight; you have to ease up on your grip in order for the blessings to get through. My mother would say to me, "Before you go to bed at night, give all your troubles to God. He is going to be up all night anyway." Try God; He is simply awesome. My parents always made my life richer beyond years. I didn't understand it so much back then, but I fully understand what they were saying today.

During my correctional officer career, in 1990, I was called up and served in Operation Desert Storm / Desert Shield conflict with the 514th Military Police Company. My military career was once again continuing. That's the one thing about being a soldier: You never know when a conflict will arise, but you always have to be ready when you are notified when such an incident has occurred. I am thankful that I had a job that, when I returned back home from the conflict, it would still be there for me. War is one thing much like our day-to-day challenges: very unpredictable but very real in reality. Just like everything else that I face in life, I pray about it and let the will of God take its place. I learned that a strong religious foundation will carry you and bring you safely down the many trails in life. God wants to see if we will truly have that faith "of a mustard seed" as we live our lives every day. There are many situations put in our pathways just to test our strength and our beliefs in God. If you look back after a lot of things have passed by, you see that God was with us all along, even though at times it seemed like He was not there. But He was all along! I wasn't always this strong in my faith and beliefs, but one day I took a good look over my life and I saw how God brought me through the many obstacles that I had been through. I never let a day go by now without praising His name. Thank Him for what God has done for me.

After Desert Storm / Desert Shield ended, and I returned back home, I decided that I wanted to do some volunteer work with the youth in my community. I saw a lot of young people coming through the correctional system and law enforcement system as a whole, making bad decisions. Choices, chances, and consequences are very important elements in our society now and definitely in the future. I felt that I wanted to be able to make a big difference with our young people. So many of our young people are misguided in the wrong directions. I started volunteering at the local Boys Club at that time. Just coming into the Boys Club, talking to the young men of our futures, can really make a difference. So many young people have such peer pressures going on in their lives, and some of them feel that they have no one that they can come to and talk about what's going on with them. That can be a very large weight that they are carrying on their shoulders. It can also be a recipe for making a bad or hasty decision. I felt as having a substantial amount of law enforcement experience now that I could maybe share a word or two and guide a young person in the right direction if they might be traveling in the wrong direction. Growing up in the city, you see that these streets are eager to snatch up those vulnerable young people. We as adults need to try our best to see that that doesn't take place. A simple "Hello," "What's happening, man?" "How was your day today?" greetings can really make a difference.

Society is constantly changing, just as the years are moving along as well. We as adults have to guide our young people through a pathway that would lead our young people to success and fulfilling future responsibilities. There are many obstacles and pitfalls along the way, but with good family values and good guidance, that young person would be able to cross that finish line to success. Every generation needs to continually pass on to the next generation what it takes to make a difference. Yes, it won't be easy but very rewarding after conquering the many challenges before you. That's when I always felt that God was right there beside me, piloting my life's pathway. In many cases, there were lucrative opportunities before me, but God would put in my spirit that that opportunity was not the one for me. After moving on to something else, I would see clearly the message that God was sending to me through a previous opportunity that I thought was good for me, and it wasn't. Let God guide you and he will take you down the right pathways that you are to follow. In other cases, man might try to discourage you in ways that really would require you putting much trust in God. Remember this, a person might build the biggest wall in front of you that you have ever seen, full of much cement that no man would appear could knock this wall down, but no wall, no cement, can stop God from breaking through any obstacles. Whatever God has for you, He will give you that opportunity to achieve what he has for you.

I lecture a lot of young people today on many things. Past experiences really help me understand and pass on some future guidance that could be helpful for someone else. As we are getting older and going through life, there are some very terrible pitfalls that may be waiting out there for you to fall into. For example, growing up or simply just hanging out in the streets of the neighborhood has many temptations. As young adults, you have to be able to make decisions whether you are going to participate in the things going on before you or make a decision not to participate in what might be going on. In many cases, you should ask yourself if your parents would be happy with the decisions you are about to make. Let that decision be a good one, one that your parents or family members would be proud of. People around you might try to steer you in the wrong directions, but that's when you might have to stand alone and simply walk away from them. Always keep your head up high and make everyone who loves you proud. Peer pressure can really be something at times; that's when you rise above and make that choice that seems so difficult at that time. Life is not always simple and easy, but through the guidance of God, He will see you through whatever you are going through. Whether it's your parents or grandparents, in most cases, you always want to keep that window of communication open. So many young people are misguided by negative influences. That's when you really can appreciate your parents or grandparents, from whom you can get the truth in most cases.

One Saturday morning, bright and early before sunrise, my telephone began ringing. I answered the phone, and it was the institution alerting me of a prison escape. I responded to the staff member that I was en route to the institution as soon as I hung up the phone. Upon my arrival at the institution, I was made aware of two inmates who had escaped from the institution. All management staff, on the different levels, as well as the appropriate outside community agencies, were made aware of the escape. One thing about working in corrections is you never know when an escape might occur; therefore, you must always be security conscious. Inmates constantly think about how they might be able to leave a facility or even how they might be able to hurt an individual. Thanks to quick responses from all parties involved, both inmates were apprehended in a relatively short period of time, without any staff members or inmates being injured. That's always a blessing for things to turn out the way they did. I always pray early in the morning, sometimes through the daytime, but surely before I turn in for bed at night. Law enforcement is a very dangerous job. When you begin your day, you never know, as an officer, what you are going to encounter for that day; therefore, in my personal opinion, you need to always keep prayer on the table. It only takes a few brief seconds for you to run into a lifetime-changing situation. I've been blessed not to have had many injuries, but I have had a few. Having a lifetime of law enforcement as a career, it's likely, more often than not, that sustaining injuries would come.

Friday afternoon while sitting in my office, a call came across on the radio about an inmate being assaulted by several other inmates on one of the housing units. All available staff immediately responded, including myself. When I arrived at the unit, several inmates had homemade knives in their hands, stabbing another inmate as he was trying to get away from the attack. Blood was everywhere. As other staff members were arriving on the scene, I was trying to ascertain who was directly involved now and also attended to who was injured. I called for immediate medical staff because I had one inmate stabbed several times in his chest and head areas. We quickly subdued the necessary inmates who were involved and removed them from the unit. It's always important to always maintain law, order, and security. The injured were placed on a stretcher, taken to our medical department, and then to the local hospital for further medical treatment. Assaults of this nature are prevalent in the prison setting. Staff members, in most instances, are always outnumbered by the prisoners, but you still can't let that stop you from doing your job that you were trained to do. At times, it's very difficult, but I did the best to my ability to make sure that staff members were able to handle themselves and control all situations that would happen. In this particular incident, the inmate who was stabbed several times was treated and released at the hospital. He was returned to the prison, where he is still serving time. The prisoners involved in the assault have had additional time added to their original sentences.

Time is just one factor that you just don't have a lot of when responding to and handling the many incidents that can occur whether you are working as a police officer on the streets or a correctional officer in the confines of a prison. You have to constantly make sure that you are following policies and procedures that you were trained to do. Therefore, you must continually study, study, and continue to always study. Laws constantly change all the time. With the help of well-trained supervisors, you'll make good decisions in your performance as an officer or even up to an administrator or perhaps a chief of a police department. Very hard work will get you across that finish line. Understanding is another factor that is needed in the law enforcement field. There is no situation that you will encounter that is 100 percent the only way to handle something, within the policy book. God gives you common sense as well. The more experience you get, the better officer you will be. Decisions after the fact. Whatever actions you take have reactions or bad consequences. So before you react to something, you have to, as quickly as possible, make a decision that this is really what you want to do. The average incident that I have ever seen happens in a matter of seconds. No matter what incidents you go through, someone stands a great chance of being hurt, whether physically, mentally, or emotionally.

CHAPTER 7

How Quickly Your Life Can Change

Loss of My Father

In 2001, it started out for me as being a very nice year. We all don't know how quickly our lives can change. I've heard this statement many times: "You should try to live each day as if it was your last." We can be up on our feet today, and so down in bed on our backs tomorrow. So please don't take life for granted. Growing up through the years from birth, adolescence, young adult, to grown-up, before you blink your eyes that fast, you would have passed through each one of these steps. To all young people: Be able to carry that successful torch by the time you come into being a grown-up. Hopefully, young people will have a role model that will help teach them, guide them, and even criticize them when needed. I was very fortunate and blessed enough to have that role model in my life. That role model was my father. He always had a strong word of encouragement, an easy word of comfort, an intellectual word for something that I was trying to accomplish. I looked at him as my right-hand man. He loved my mother dearly. He also taught me how to be an independent man.

In October of 2007, my father was in the hospital. Doctors ran a variety of tests on him because he just wasn't feeling well. They kept him for a few days while they were running tests. After a few days, the doctors could not find anything abnormal, so they decided that they were going to let him be released back home. That evening when I went over to see him in the hospital, my mother and son were already visiting with him. After we were finishing visiting with him, we were getting ready to go home for the day because I was going to pick him up the next day after he was released from the hospital. As I was about to close the door, leaving from his room, my father called me over to him and said to me, "If anything were to ever happen to me, make sure that you take care of your number 1 (your mother) and your family as well."

I said to him, "Surely I would always do that, but I'll be over here early tomorrow in order to bring you home." I then left the hospital and drove home. I was home about thirty minutes when my telephone rang. When I said hello, my mother was on the other end crying very frantically. My mother said to me that my father had just died. My father had a major stroke within thirty minutes after I left the hospital, which he did not recover from. Briefly, I was in total shock. My world had turned so upside down so quickly. I quickly went to my parents' home where my mother, son, and other family members were gathering as they heard the shocking news. Losing a parent was a hard pill for me to swallow, literally. I've had some very hard bumps and bruises in my life before, but this was a very hard time now in my life. My father and I were very close. I had no secrets from him, no matter what. Honesty across the board. I always remembered what he asked me to do before he passed, and that was to take care of my mother and family. And I did just that. My father taught me how to take care of all the business aspects of life as if he was here himself. I thank him for putting in one thing that I don't think you could ever prepare yourself for, even if you tried.

It changes your life completely. You'll never get over the loss of that loved one, but you learn how to live with it. You get stronger every day and you learn how to put the loss of a loved one into perspective. God is in control all the time, no matter what we are going through. The roads may appear to be very tough at times, but through it all, God is always there. In the midst of any storm, calm seas will soon appear to be no way possible. Different events happen in our lives, at many times, but that's God giving us a test, a test to see just how much faith we will have in him. Whatever we are going through, God already has the answer. If we just learn how to lean and depend on Jesus, everything will be alright. I have so many great memories of my father and I. Many days I just picture him looking down on me, just smiling. It gives me great inner peace to know how much of an impact my father made on my life. He impacted me the way that I want to impact my own son's life. Obstacles will come and go, but I want my son to be able to ask such questions as, "What would my father do in this situation?" or "How would he respond to these challenges before me?" Before he would make his decisions, let it be one that was carefully thought out before he responded. It's been quite a few years now since my father passed away, but there is not a day that goes by that I don't look up at his picture and get a pleasant smile on my face. There are also times that I will sit down in my living room and put one of his sermons in the cassette player, just to hear his voice. He surely lived the life that he preached.

Not many days would go by that I didn't hear my mother say, "I sure do miss your father." There was much love shown in our home while growing up, which is very transparent in my home today. I often would take my mother out to lunch or dinners at her favorite restaurants. It was very important to me, for me to make sure that she could live her life as content as possible and that she didn't have to worry about expenses of any sort. My parents did for me while growing up, and now it was time for me to do for her. As the days went along, things seemed to get a little calmer. Thank God for that.

During these days, I also balanced out the beginning of my dog business. I always loved animals, but growing up in New York City, certain places where we lived just didn't have the appropriate space for pets. I had the space now that I needed, and I started my K-9 business of raising Akitas. That was a breed of dog that originated from Japan. A dog that was very intelligent, loyal, and protective. My mother selected my first Akita, a male dog solid white in color and with a very gentle temperament. We named him Scrappy-Doo, from the *Scooby-Doo* cartoon characters. I also got two female dogs, Akitas as well, Duchess and Princess. Duchess was an American Akita, and Princess was a Japanese Akita. Scrappy-Doo was an Inu Akita. He grew very large. A lot of people referred to him as the Bear Dog. He maxed out in weight at 156 pounds, but still, he was very gentle. All the dogs became like members of the family as well.

Raising, training, and breeding the dogs was very good for the family. My mother, as well as my son, took a very active part in helping me with the business. It was very demanding at times, but also rewarding down the road. To be successful in whatever you venture out into will require hard work, patience, and dedication. Most of all, I prayed for a successful beginning and let God take us through the good and hard times, so prayerfully we would have successful endings. I was always raised and taught that no matter what you do, put God first. We take a lot of things for granted and we shouldn't. When you start to look back through the years, you see that many people are leaving this world all the time. It starts trickling down that not only do you recognize it from watching the news on TV, but you see it within your own communities that you live in.

Many elderly people in our communities really did an awesome job paving the way through society for the next generations to come. I really appreciated those communities that made those sacrifices for me to have opportunities to succeed in the future. A lot of the next generation, no doubt, gets wiser but, in a lot of cases, refuses to listen or perhaps learn from those who have traveled that way before them. In turn, that makes them weaker. We have to pass the torch on to the next generation if we are to ever have good success. Too many young people are going down the wrong road for no good reason. Surely, young people are going through different stages in life, but they need to make better decisions, those decisions that won't end them up in going to jail, prison, or even some causing their deaths. It's very important to be in our children's lives. From day to day, a lot of things are going on with our children. Being able to talk to someone (that will give good guidance) can really make a difference. Suicides and crime are at an all-time high. A lot of these incidents can be avoided, but we all must play a part to make these changes for these incidents not to happen. One life lost is one life too many. One crime that is committed is also one person locked up for a senseless crime that should have never even happened. You see, we can make changes, but it has to be a group effort. I personally do quite a few lectures to young people because it's very important to help them with knowledge and experiences. We have to be determined in order to make a difference.

As the years are today, our young people just live for the moment, in most cases. The future is not even on the radar. Our forefathers would probably wonder where they possibly went wrong. They didn't go wrong. It's just that the upcoming generation just didn't want to receive the messages that were sent to them. My grandparents, as well as my parents, worked very hard. There were no silver spoons put into my mouth. The lessons, the hard work, and experiences are what it would take for me to succeed.

I love cooking, barbecuing, and simply frying fish on my back porch in my big deep fryer. I also enjoy going to the movies, art shows, museums, and the zoo. To relax after a long day, I love my music. R&B, jazz, gospel, and classical are some of my favorites. Luther Vandross, Teddy Pendergrass, Freddie Jackson, Peabo Bryson, and please don't forget Patti LaBelle, Aretha Franklin, Gladys Knight, Whitney Houston, and Stephanie Mills. I enjoy traveling, reading, and writing. Through it all, I definitely do make time for going to church and worshiping God. Because of God, He makes it all possible for me and everything that I even attempt to do. My parents always instilled in me the importance of keeping that thought in my mind and never forgetting what God has done for me and continues to do for me. I've met a lot of people throughout my career. For the most part, they were good people, but just as anything else that you go through, there were people in your pathway not traveling down the same journey.

It's a proven fact that sometimes you just have to stand alone. At times, it can be hard and even painful, but as long as you know what's right, you stand strong on your principles. Law enforcement is a very complex career. There are many factors that you have to learn, especially if you are going to make a career out of it.

Policies, procedures and punishments are very different from state to state even if you are considering the same offensives. Your instructors, teachers, and counselors, however you define them, are very essential to your success. Over a period of time, you will learn (hopefully) how to apply the different laws (that you have been taught about) to many situations that you will encounter. There are no two of the same days when working in the criminal justice field. There are millions of people in this country. When you think that you have seen everything, there's always something new. I found out for myself that I had to find a release valve for the things that I might go through at work. Work was work. Being home is where you need to relax. I learned how to keep them separated. That's how I was able to keep that stress out of my life. As a policeman, you had access to moving around within the community in which you are working, but when working in correctional setting? You don't have as much freedom (to move around) as you did as a police officer. In corrections, your movement is restricted to the prison's confines. So actually, you, as a staff member, are doing time just as the offenders you are supervising are doing their sentences for their crimes in which they have been sentenced. Having a stress reliever is very important. I volunteer in the community in which I live and within the surrounding counties as well. I believe that it is very important to give back to your communities.

That's just another part of rebuilding the new generations. Keep the young people busy with work, school, family chores, and anything else (legally and productive) to form a positive influence in society. As the old saying says, "An idle mind is the devil's workshop." Staying busy is a good way of keeping people out of a lot of trouble. I coached several soccer teams throughout the years as well as I went on all the field trips that my son went on while he was in school. I felt that it was very necessary to be a parent who was very engaged in what was going on with your children (while in school) and even after school. Raising children is a full-time job. There's always something new and challenging going on with your children. It's good to be supportive of everything that is important to them. We as parents, no doubt, won't agree with everything children explore with, but we need to always take an interest in whatever they are doing as much as possible. When (as a parent) we show a lack of interest toward our children, that intel opens up the opportunity for misguidance and bad decision-making. Peer pressure can skyrocket a lot of trouble. Love and attendances can help our young people go a long way.

Through my years as working in law enforcement, I've seen many cases of good people turning to bad things. The world is changing all the time, but you have to be strong and not let the bad things change you or the young ones in society. One bad decision that you make can cause a lifetime of pain. When everything seems to be going very good in your life. Those times are drawing negatively as well. Some people just do not like to see another person succeed. That's when you have to rise up and be even that much stronger. What's that familiar saying that "misery does love company." Rise up, be strong, and make a difference. Reach back and pull that person who might be trying to get where you just left and teach them the way. It's easy to put on a uniform, but it takes a lot of dedication to wear it right. The thin line (of officers) truly runs deep. I say to my fellow brothers that I am so proud and thankful to be a member. I've been blessed enough to serve on many different levels, and I give all my thanks to God. Without God, there would have been no career or any other type of success. Thank you, God, for what you have done in my life. I give him all the honor and praise. Leaving your home, going to work, You never know what situations you are going to face. In many situations, you could easily get injured or, in some situations, even lose your life. Therefore, you definitely need to keep God in the plan. Your life can change in the blink of an eye.

I watched several officers struggle with coping with the day-to-day many different incidents. Whether being in military basic training, police officer academy, or correctional officer basic training, they all give you a brief overview of the incidents that you might face, but the real test will be when those incidents happen, and now you have to make split decisions in dealing with the incidents. That's when your training and experiences will now be applied. In many cases, it will also show a lot of officers if this career is really one that they want to remain in for the duration. Law enforcement is a very demanding career. It requires great dedication. Incontrovertible hours and little appreciation at times, but a great reward if you stick with it. "To protect and to save speaks volumes right by itself. Laws of the land change all the time, but without laws, we would have a very disastrous society. In spite of the severe consequences that breaking today's laws will bring out, criminal justice system is still at an all-time high. People's morals have changed greatly. They seem not to care if they made that bad decision and committed that bad crime. For a lot of people? Going to jail or prison is a sinful pastime to them these days. We as a society have to find ways to disencourage our young people (and others) from making these bad choices. The consequences are too high and severe. If we all just take it one day at a time, one person at a time, we possibly can make a big difference, if we all, as a society, just try.

CHAPTER 8

Memorable Events

I remember the beautiful spring day when I took my son to the local park, as I so often did. While at the park, he ran and played around on the various equipment that was there. It had swing sets, things he could climb on, and also the monkey bars. There was also a straight metal bar attached to the bars that you climbed on. I decided that I would show my son a trick that I used to do when I was his age and went to the park. I first grabbed the bar with my hands, and then I flipped over (upside down) and put my feet on the bar where my hands originally were. I could balance my whole body, hanging with my feet. After a few seconds, I flipped back over to my hands and my original position. Then I decided to hold my body up on the bar with one hand suspended. That's when my arm just snapped. I immediately fell to the ground. A public works worker, who was working around in the park at the time, saw me fall. He ran over to me and assisted me to my feet. I asked him to help me get to my car. He did. I was in a lot of pain, but I drove myself and my son to my parents' house (they lived very close by). My son was too small to drive at that time, so I did have to drive, and I made it. I kept looking at my arm because it was just throbbing, and I thought that the bone was going to come through the skin at any moment. It never did, but it sure hurt a lot. When my son and I made it to my parents' house, my son jumped out of the car (after I stopped) and ran to my parents' house and began ringing the doorbell. My father came to the door, and my son said to my father that I was hurt inside of my car.

My father and mother came outside. Then my father took me in his car to the local hospital because I needed some emergency care now. When I got to the Emergency Department at the local hospital, the hospital personnel immediately took me back into the treatment area. That's when an orthopedic surgeon came into my room after viewing my X-rays and told me that I had ruptured my biceps and that they needed to do emergency surgery to repair the damage within my arm. I was totally stunned. I was looking for the doctor to come into the room, wrap my arm in a bandage, tell me that I had a very bad sprain, and then send me home. Not the complete opposite, but he did. The next morning after surgery was the beginning road to recovery. The doctor informed me that repairing the torn bicep was a success, but that it would take me approximately six to nine months of physical therapy and rehab to get my arm back to its strength and recovery. In all actuality, it took exactly that long. At that time, I was a superintendent in corrections, assigned to supervising a segregation unit. I had to switch over to Administrative duties due to the nature of my injury. When we have the use of our limbs from day to day, we take a lot of things for granted. When you are restricted in the use of different limbs, things become very challenging at times. Thanks to good physical therapy, my arm healed and became even stronger than it was before the injury. God often puts challenging tasks in front of us, but just stay strong and lean on Him, and whatever you are going through, He will see you through to the end.

A lot of times, we (as people) will judge people on situations without knowing all the facts. In many cases, another person might not even give you an explanation, but before you start saying something that you might regret later, you need to find out what know factual about something, before you start saying something that you can't take back once it's been said. Our tongue can be a terrible weapon at times. You can lash something out, but you might not have enough time to get it back in. I could be sitting down in a chair, and all of a sudden, I would just drop off to sleep. I got to a point where if I was fast to sleep at night (in bed), I would wake up from my sleep gasping (trying to catch my breath). I later found out that I had *sleep apnea*. I was given several machines that I was supposed to use to help me with breathing. It helped me to sleep better, but I knew that there had to be something else that I could do, for me to get better. The doctors also said that exercise and a different diet could help also. A good friend of mine gave me a very good dietary plan. She went through all the food groups with me. She told me what to eat, how much to eat, and definitely things to stay away from. I followed her dietary plan to a tee. I lost a considerable amount of weight. My blood pressure and glucose changed dramatically for the better. I felt a lot better, and my sleep apnea and all its symptoms went away. My good friend gave me a lifeline that I stick to very much to the day.

Habachi steak, Habachi chicken, carrots, broccoli, hamburger, fish, salads, vegetables in general, and blueberries and blackberries is a winning start to losing weight and keeping it off successfully. Losing weight is truly a lifestyle change. You have to be committed that this is really what you want to do. For me, living is enough motivation for me to take on this task. I also went from drinking a lot of sodas then to drinking water, with Crystal Light mixes added to it. These small changes have given me a very worthwhile outcome. Some people have good results in counting calories or perhaps reading labels on whatever they are buying. That process was too time-consuming for me. I had to grab hold of a system that was very workable for me. Try a few things, then apply them to your diet as it is working for you. Take baby steps before you start walking. Then walk a little while before you start running. Apply this same format to any diet that you are trying out as a newcomer. I've never been a traditional diet type person. Doing everything is not going to work for everybody. My best suggestion is working it out through trial and error. There's an old saying, "Nothing beats a failure but a try." So try, try, try, and make it happen for you. Carbs are a big no-no for all of us because there are a lot of carbs in most of the things that we like to eat. Be mindful and limit your carb intake. Pizza, spaghetti, lasagna, I'm a big fan, but they have a lot of carbs in your intake. Be careful and remember that there is nothing wrong with eating something every now and then in moderation.

Thinking back on the years that have passed, a lot of things have taken place. The majority of things have been good memories, but just like anything else that happens, many storms will come your way. I truly believe that God designs things that way so that we would never stop appreciating Him. God has been so patient with us. Even when we make our mistakes, He is still so humble and merciful to forgive us for whatever we have done and asked forgiveness for. Having God in your life is a process of changing the things that you might be doing in your life for the good. Just as being a law enforcement officer, the longer you work in the field, through time and experience, you should grow and become a good officer. Some officers like to take shortcuts and adhere to the wrong temptations in front of them. Those wrong temptations will cause you to hit that ultimate "back wall." I call it the wall of destruction. That's why it is so important to keep God in the plan. We can't do anything just by ourselves and hope to remain successful. You have to put God in the mix. I just can't say that enough. My mother used to constantly say, "Treat people right and nice around you. Even if at times they treat you wrong, you still treat them right." Let God fight your battles, not you. God will work them out to perfection, every time. In a twenty-eight-year career, you are going to work with all types of people. So you have to prepare yourself for all types of very different personalities.

CHAPTER 9

The Loss of My Mother

At birth, you immediately have that connection, like no other connection, with your mother and then with your father. They give you that sense of feeling warm and secure. You as a young child have no worry. Your parents absorb all the situations that would come before you. They teach us their ways so that one day after we grow up, we would have matured to the point that we would be able to take care of our own families. It's a process that fathers have to teach their sons how to be independent men, and mothers have to teach their daughters how to be good women.

It was now the year of 2012. Just as in other years in the past, it was work, taking care of my mother and family, and trying to enjoy life as best as possible. This one particular day, I called my mother from work, just to check on her and see how her day was going. In talking with her over the telephone, something just seemed a little different in her voice. It seemed a little slurred. I decided that I needed to leave work and physically go and check on her. My spirit was just uneasy about how she sounded on the phone during our conversation. When I arrived at her house, as I entered the house, I met Scrappy-Doo inside the house at the door. He was our large Akita that stayed over at my mother's house. He was truly her guard dog. For the most part, he was trained to stay outside, unless there was an emergency inside the house that involved my mother. So I knew by him being in the house, something had to be wrong.

54

He backed up from me and turned around as if he wanted me to follow him. He went straight to my mother's bedroom, where she was lying across her bed very weak. When I looked at her, I could see that her mouth had started to turn, and her speech was really slurred. I knew that these were signs of a person having or having had a stroke. I put Scrappy back outside as I immediately had already called for the rescue squad. When the rescue squad transported my mother to the emergency room, the doctor's diagnosis was that my mother had had several mini-strokes earlier that day. My mother stayed very sick in the hospital for a while.

While in the hospital, she had some heart complications as well. After staying in the hospital for about four weeks, my mother was sent to a rehab center, where she stayed another three weeks. I was back and forth from the rehab center two to three times a day, and back and forth to the office at work. I finally decided to take off from work completely for a while. My mother was very sick, and she needed me more than ever now. My parents are always more important than any job. God will guide you and keep you if you only have faith and believe. He will surely make ways out of no ways, as we see as impossible. My mother seemed like she was getting better each day at the rehab center, so she was going to be released the next day, and I was going to pick her up and bring her home. That being said, I decided to go back to work. As I entered the lobby that morning, the switchboard operator notified me that I had an emergency outside call.

My mother was being rushed back to the hospital from the rehab center. When I got to the hospital and finally saw my mother, she was up in the heart center (she had had a heart attack). She stayed in the heart center for a total of twenty-one days. I was back and forth from the heart center. While she was in the heart center, my mother began singing one of her favorite songs, "If I Can Help Somebody, Then My Living Will Not Be in Vain."

If I can help somebody, as I travel long?
If I can cheer somebody with a word or a song?
If I can show somebody that he's traveling wrong?
Then my living shall not, be in vain.

As I was sitting in her hospital room, she just sang, and periodically she would say to me, "Kelvin, it's going to be alright." I knew then that my mother was at peace as to whatever God was getting ready to do in her life. My mother believed in praying and fasting, and so do I. Whatever you may have a question about, take it to the Lord, and he will make it clear that you will understand what he is saying to you. I went home from the hospital in order to change my clothes. When I returned back, to the hospital, my mother had skipped off into a coma. I never heard my mother speak to me again.

I say this to all people who have a living grandparent, father, mother, or person who raised you. Go over to them often, throw your arms around them, and tell them how much you love them and how much they mean to you. In all cases, somebody did for us when we could not do for ourselves.

My mother now being in a coma, I still went over to the hospital and just sat by her side and talked to her. One evening, March 7, around 7:00 p.m., while I was in my mother's room, I stood up to change the TV channel on the television at the same time that the nurse ran into the room (and passed by my sister) and began doing chest compressions because my mother had flat-lined. I didn't want to see this procedure being done on my mother, so I came out of the room while the medical staff tried to revive my mother. They were unsuccessful in reviving her; my mother had just died! The queen in my life had just left this world. It's been very hard and very difficult at times. You never get over losing a parent; you just learn to live with it from day to day. Death is so hard, but as sure as we are living, we all one day have to close our eyes. There's no way around doing that. I look at my parents' pictures every day on the walls in my home, and they always make me __ because I have such good memories. They instilled in me a strong religious foundation. One thing that I remember constantly is to not put your trust in man (because man will let you down). You need to put your trust in God. God will see you through, whatever you are going through.

It has been some years now since I lost both of my parents, but the wounds are just as fresh as if it just happened yesterday. As I have said earlier? I truly do look forward to seeing all my family members and friends one day again on the other side. I returned to work for a few months after my mother passed. Then at the end of the year, I decided that I would retire. It was time for me to put an end to a good beginning. Writing this book has been very rewarding to me in many ways. I want to thank everyone who has shared many words of wisdom to me down through the years. Your guidance has really impacted my life. There have been too many individuals for me to begin to name. Those of you whom I know personally, you know my heart, and you know the person that I am. I'll always appreciate and thank you for everything that you have done for me. May God continue to bless us all and keep us. Amen.

Kelvin Daniels
To God be the glory.

State of North Carolina
Certificate of Retirement
Presented to
Kelvin Daniels
The State of North Carolina acknowledges and extends its sincere
ated service.
Agency Head
Governor